God Bless Women

Palmwine Sounds

PALMWINE PUBLISHING

Copyright © 2024 Palmwine Publishing Limited Nigeria

All rights reserved. No part of this publication may be reproduced, distributed, or transmitted in any form or by any means, including photocopying, recording, or other electronic or mechanical methods, without the prior written permission of the publisher, except in the case of brief quotations embodied in critical reviews and certain other non-commercial uses permitted by copyright law.

Author- Palmwine Sounds

Illustrations- Kehinde Omotosho

ISBN (Paperback)- 978-1-917267-00-7
ISBN (E-Book)- 978-1-917267-01-4

Published by Nubian Republic Ltd UK on behalf of Palmwine Publishing Nigeria Limited

Email: info@palmwinepublishing.com

Address- UK: 86-90, Paul Street, London EC2A 4NE

Address-Nigeria: 1A Jos Road Bukuru, Plateau State, Nigeria.

www.palmwinepublishing.com

www.raffiapress.com

www.nuciferaanalysis.com

ABOUT BOOK - GOD BLESS WOMEN

"God Bless Women" is a captivating poetry collection that celebrates the strength, resilience, and beauty of women. Through poignant verses and heartfelt prose, this collection explores the power and grace of women in all their forms. From the fierce warrior to the gentle nurturer, each poem pays tribute to the incredible spirit of women everywhere. Join us on a journey of empowerment, inspiration, and gratitude as we honour and uplift the divine essence of women in this remarkable collection.

YANSH

A beautiful material property
I see it and appreciate it.
Bring am, make I lie down.
Small yansh shakes, everyone pauses.
Big yansh shakes, everyone is in a trance.
Scenes are created in my head.
I can't be blamed, I am just a man.
When it circulates, another go penetrate
If it was a religion, heaven is assured.

BREAST

A natural stress ball and fidget
Squeezing it eases the stress.
Playing with the switch
Up, down, pull, twist...
It gets hard to appreciate.

AUNTS

An extension of your mother
They pamper you like a king or queen.
Calling you fine boy or girl until your head swells.
Mum turns her head, lips squeezed pointing upward.
In disagreement with mum, you cry to them.
Finding a middle ground, so peace can reign.
Tell you stories of your family history.
My mum did that, you say to her.

GRANDMOTHER

We miss you. Mother cries at night, I know nothing I say would comfort her. So, I ignore it. Knowing only you can comfort her even if you are not here.

I miss breaking and tying firewood to sell.
Miss, helping you cook, teaching me great cooking skills I appreciate today.
Fighting on getting me a fair wage for work I did.

I miss your parables and wise words, of which as I get older, I look back and say; "ohh! now I understand".
If there is a heaven, I know you are there dancing with the angels.

GOD BLESS WOMEN-PALMWINE SOUNDS

GOD BLESS WOMEN-PALMWINE SOUNDS

BLACK QUEENS

My black queens come in different shades, from the blackest black to the whitest black.

My Igbo queens standing tall with pride, the saying, better soup nah money kill am.

My Hausa Fulani queens, as beautiful as the cloudless desert sky.

My Plateau queens, creating a home of peace, while killing me with healthy meals.

My Yoruba queens would add pepper to your life.

My Ghanaian queens, IKEBE SUPER!!! Jiggle jiggle, up and down it goes.

My Somalian queens, beauty reflecting the gaze of the moon and the sun.

My Gambian queens, sweet accents that is comforting.

My Senegalese queens, creating well-tailored outfits.

My Congolese queens, preparing flesh of different types and formats.

My South African queens, nyash supported by leg work, attract the kings.

My Rwandan queens, tight waist with nyash to support.

My Ethiopian and Eritrean queens, beauty that perplex.

My Kenyan queens, having great endurance and stamina.

My Sudanese queens, beauties shooting to the clouds.

My Zimbabwean queens, with a beautiful sense of humour.

My Moroccan and Egyptian queens, eyes that flatter, make knees weak.

My Caribbean queens, instilling self-discipline, morals, and values into the young.

GOD BLESS WOMEN-PALMWINE SOUNDS

WOMEN'S WORLD

This is a man's world
A statement far from the truth
Women create children.
Women mould boys into men
Women can cause wars.
Women are a source of comfort.
Women are a source of strength.
Women make a castle a home.
The strongest of men have strong women.
The biggest thug, respect his mother.
Every man needs queens and princess going to the extreme for them.

POLYGAMY DREAMS

I too like women,
Or maybe I am just an ashawo.
But ashawo nah management.
Baba Fela on the beat.
Rema spoke it, I felt it.
More women more wahala,
I want the wahala.
Go into the world and multiply!
Some took it more seriously.
Women to the left of me,
Women to the right of me,
Black, white, yellow, brown....
African, Asian, European, American...
Skinny, fat, tall, short...
Small or big, Nyash or Breast,
I want them all.
Pampering me like a King,
I reciprocate by treating as Queens.

GOD BLESS WOMEN-PALMWINE SOUNDS

SWEET MOTHER

Tap, tap, in the middle of the night.
She gets the hint.
In flask, boiling water awaits.
She scoops me Milo and milk.
Adds sugar to my taste.
I drink to my satisfaction.
Back to la-la land I go.
As she tucks me in bed, laying beside me.

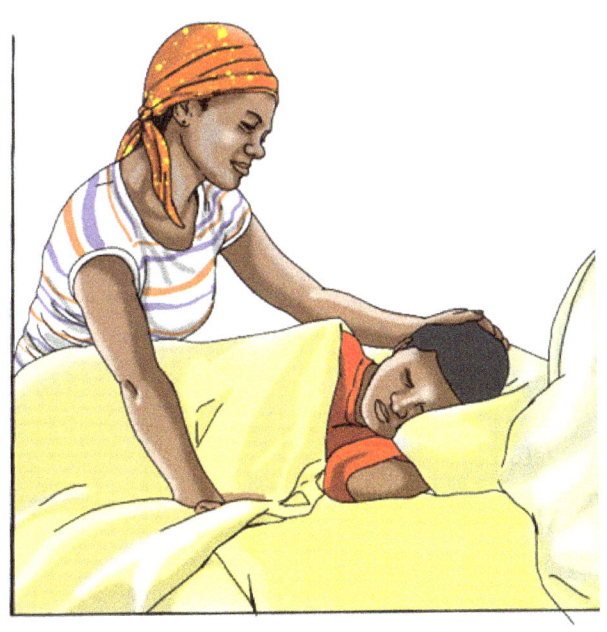

THIGHS

Pillows from heaven,
Warm and comforting.
Lay my head on it,
All problem disappears.
Head in-between,
Suffocate me.
What a glorious exit,
My ancestor would be proud.

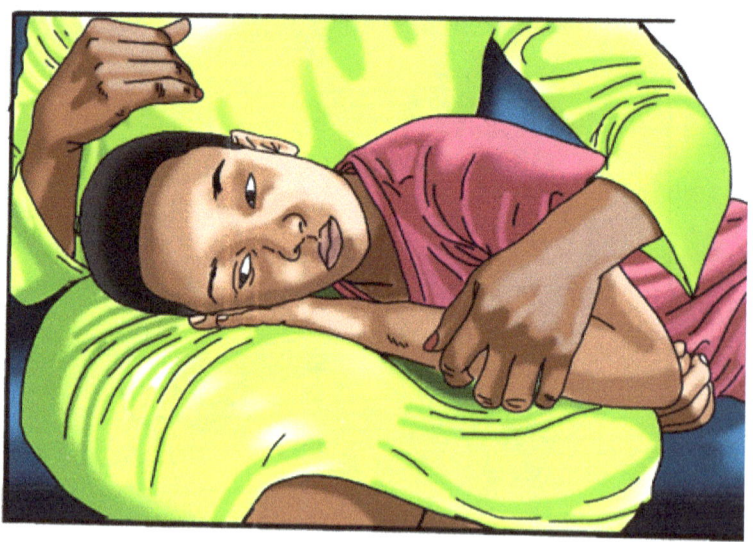

SISTERS

The mosquito's song begins.
Headache and high temperature are the effects.
The annoying pest running around fighting like Bruce Lee.
Food, Water, Medicine, she brings to my side.
TV remote we always fight for is now in my position.
Is this the same person am always fighting with?.
A sister's love is pure and true.

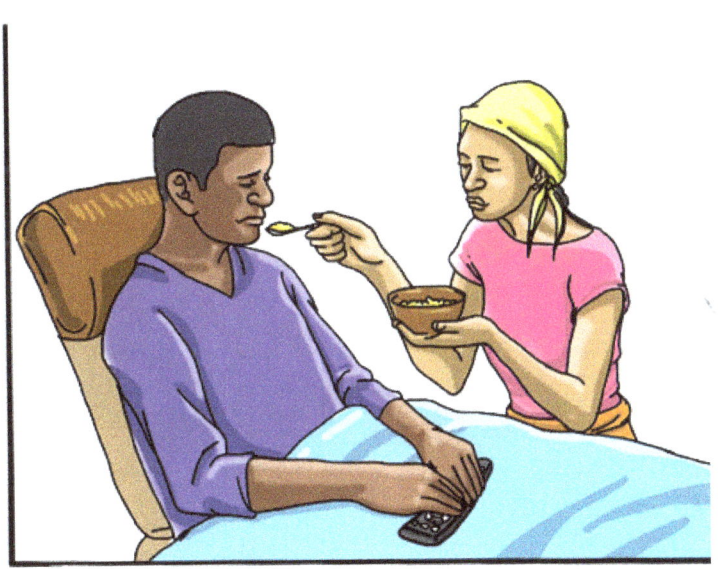

TOTO

Remove the packaging.
Squeeze the two warm loaves.
Oil it in preparation to feast.
Using my knife to cut down the middle.
Before sliding it in and out.
Till we are both satisfied.

WIVES

In Genesis it says rib, which can also be translated as life or side.
In Ephesians it says submit, which can also be translated to support.
In Proverbs it says, 'he who finds a wife finds a good thing'.
Darwin weighed the cons and pros of a wife, and pros won.
In Al-Baqarah it says, 'Your spouses are a garment for you as you are for them'.
In Al-A'raf, it says, 'It is He who created you from one soul and created from it its mate that he might dwell in security with her'.
Married men I leave you this you. Take your time and compose something for your wife(s). Give some ammunition.

GOD BLESS WOMEN-PALMWINE SOUNDS

GOD BLESS WOMEN-PALMWINE SOUNDS

GOD BLESS WOMEN-PALMWINE SOUNDS

Notes

'Thay may peper and solt it as they plese'
— **Timothy Dexter**

www.ingramcontent.com/pod-product-compliance
Lightning Source LLC
Chambersburg PA
CBHW070850160426
43192CB00012B/2388